Able To Bear It

By Gertrude Grace Sanborn

THE BIBLE FOR TODAY PUBLISHERS
900 Park Avenue
Collingswood, New Jersey 08108

Able To Bear It

By Gertrude Grace Sanborn

THE BIBLE FOR TODAY PUBLISHERS
900 Park Avenue
Collingswood, New Jersey 08108

(Originally Published By Regular Baptist Press)

Able To Bear It   By Gertrude Grace Sanborn

Published by
THE BIBLE FOR TODAY PRESS
900 Park Avenue
Collingswood, New Jersey 08108
U.S.A.

Pastor D. A. Waite, Th.D., Ph.D.

Bible For Today Baptist Church
Church Phone: 856-854-4747
BFT Phone: 856-854-4452
Orders: 1-800-John 10:9
e-mail: BFT@BibleForToday.org
Website: www.BibleForToday.org
fax: 856-854-2464

We Use and Defend
The King James Bible
April, 2014
BFT 4089
Copyright, 2014
All Rights Reserved

ISBN #978-1-56848-106-7

Cover Design and Publishing facilitated by:
The Old Paths Publications, Inc.
www.theoldpathspublications.com
706-865-0153

iv   **Able To Bear It**   By Gertrude Grace Sanborn

**The Author--Gertrude Grace Sanborn
(Mrs. R. O. Sanborn)
(1904–1988)
The picture was taken at age forty-seven.**

Preface by the Author
(Written to her daughter, Yvonne Sanborn Waite, July 29, 1980)

- A friend told my daughter that Beverly had "*made me who I am.*" I thought about those words.
- **Not only Beverly, but each child** the Lord gave me, has contributed and helped to make me what I am.
- **God has given each GIFT (child) that He loaned us**, or gave us, to make us what we are and to help frame us to be what He wants us to be.
- **The sorrows of our first dear child, Yvonne**, with her poor hip and the years and tears of it all brought us grief due to the long years of her trial. Yet, how she gladdened our hearts as she bravely went through childbearing and other hard places without whimpers.
- **Audrey, dear girl, who wanted to live, love, marry, and be a mother.** But that terrible monster "Hodgkins disease" took her strength and vigor, and slowly took her away from her parents, her sisters, and her sweetheart. We watched helplessly, not daring to weep before others.
- **Then, of course, there is Beverly**--whom most people think is our only trial. She was to have been such a delight and joy, but she became a heartache and tears beyond telling in public. She has taken over my old age and forty-five years of my life.
- **Yet, through it all, I have learned to submit to what God has allowed in our lives** until submission has become my first thought of each day and each duty.
- **Truly HE IS THE GOD OF ALL GRACE.**

1 CORINTHIANS 10:13

There hath no temptation taken you but such as is common to man: but God is faithful, who will not suffer you to be tempted above that ye are able; but will with the temptation also make a way to escape, that ye may be able to bear it.

Foreword

Years ago when REGULAR BAPTIST PRESS first published *Able to Bear It*, people with broken hearts found hope in Gertrude Sanborn's words that life could be more than just endured. It could become a blessing in spite of the constant care of a disabled, or ill child, or loved one. It is our hope and prayer with this new printing of this book that your life will be transformed by a renewed determination to serve Him as you serve your infirmed one.

For many years, *Able to Bear It* could be found only in a copy machine format. Now with the republishing of the book *by THE BIBLE FOR TODAY MINISTRIES,* it gives my husband, Dr. D. A. Waite, and me great pleasure to allow you, once more, to be blessed, comforted, and encouraged with its message. I trust that your spiritual edification, dear reader, and heart-comfort can be renewed by the Holy Spirit's using Gertrude G. Sanborn's words of wisdom, comfort, and *holy* resolve to lead you to personal victory in the difficult places of your life.

May the Lord use my mother's testimony to renew your determination to live for Him in spite of your difficulties. Your child may never be cured out of the present dilemma, nor will you be able to escape it, but you, through the patience and comfort of the Scriptures, can learn to endure the hurt and the work, as well as the rude stares from the curious who pass by your life and the life of your loved one. (I know this from personal experience). Such solace and hope can be found for you, too, as my mother discovered it many years ago. Her consolation came in a Book-- God's Book--the Bible.

Able To Bear It   By Gertrude Grace Sanborn

Many parents have children who must face life with unexplained illnesses or deformities. Often that *life of unusualness* falls on the shoulders of the parents and caregivers. The sorrows, the stares, and the aloneness is not only the child's burden, but also the parent's life challenge, too. That is why *Able to Bear It* has touched the hearts of grieving mothers, fathers, siblings, and grandparents. Gertrude Sanborn had experienced every emotion there ever was in such circumstances of life.

In writing her book, Mother remembered the stark unbelief she felt as the realization dawned on her that her little girl was not like other children. Had not the lingering years of illness of her firstborn daughter been enough? Mother's Heavenly Father, in His wisdom, permitted grief that, at first, could not be put into words. It encompassed her being with despair. In utter disbelief, Gertrude realized that her only hope for emotional survival was found in the Words of God. So, Gertrude put her whole life, and the lives of her three daughters, into God's hand (Psalm 31:15) as she daily immersed herself in God's Words! Many years later, Gertrude's second-born daughter, Audrey, died at the age of twenty from Hodgkin's disease, which, at the time, was an incurable cancer.

In the book, Gertrude Sanborn wrote the following:
Perhaps there are other ways for people to solve their problems and bear their burdens. But for the Christian, Christ is the answer. As for me, I find no answer, no place of refuge, no solution, no escape but in the Word of God as I read it and lay hold of it. It is in this Book that I see my Lord, "touched" with the feeling

of my infirmity, and I see His purpose, His power and His love for me. (*ABLE TO BEAR IT*, page 23)

From personal experience with a mentally ill son, my husband and I know the sorrows that come with such a dreadful diagnosis. I, too, know the tears, the unbelief, the despair. Always before me was my mother's example of being *able to bear it* in such overwhelming sorrow. Mother, and my father R. O. Sanborn, too, were examples of leaning on the Lord Jesus Christ and trusting the Words of God for their refuge, their daily survival, and their personal endurance. **I thank God for their testimonies and examples!**

May God, once again use Gertrude Sanborn's life and her love for the Scriptures as an example for you, dear readers. God is able in your life, in spite of such struggles, for you, too, to be *Able To Bear It* (1 Corinthians 10:13).

In God's wise care,

Yvonne Sanborn Waite
(Mrs. D. A. Waite)

[All poems in this book are by Gertrude Grace Sanborn except two which were written by Audrey June Sanborn.]

I want to thank the following people for proofreading this edition of *Able To Bear It*: Patricia Canter, Anne Marie Noyle, Tamara Waite, as well as my husband, Pastor D. A. Waite, who edited, typed the copy as well as making the extensive **INDEX.**

Able To Bear It By Gertrude Grace Sanborn

Table of Contents

Publisher's Data iii
Preface by the Author v
Foreword vii
Table of Contents xi
John 3:16-21 xiii
Able To Bear It–The Purpose Of This Book 1
To Beverly Grace Sanborn 3
1. Only A Fable 5
2. The Doctor Said 7
3. I Cried 9
    Our Gems 10
4. I Prayed 11
    The Cost 12
5. I Became Weary 13
    The Lord, Our Banner 14
6. My Friends 15
7. The Pride Of Life 17
    Grace 18
8. He Cares For Me 19
    God's Tomorrow 20
9. Knowing The Doctrine 21
    Deep In God's Word 23
10. A Way To Escape 25
    Now For A Season 27
11. How Precious 29
    Precious Problem 30
12. Shut Up To Him 31
    Learning 33
13. Recognition 35

Audrey	36
Her Empty Room	37
He Cares For Me	39
14. Comforted	41
Understanding	43
Bearing And Learning	45
15. Able To Bear It	49
A Prayer	51
Since I Learned To Trust Him	53
Why?	54
Victory	55
Appendix	57
Keep Me Looking Up	58
The Thief	59
Thank You, Lord	60
Lord, I'm Glad	61
I Wonder What It Is	62
I Alone	63
So Long	64
Just A Short Time	65
Index of Words and Phrases	67
Order Blank Pages	83
Defined King James Bible Order Form	91

JOHN 3:16-21

For God so loved the world, that he gave his only begotten Son, that whosoever believeth in him should not perish, but have everlasting life. For God sent not his Son into the world to condemn the world; but that the world through him might be saved. He that believeth on him is not condemned: but he that believeth not is condemned already, because he hath not believed in the name of the only begotten Son of God. And this is the condemnation, that light is come into the world, and men loved darkness rather than light, because their deeds were evil. For every one that doeth evil hateth the light, neither cometh to the light, lest his deeds should be reproved. But he that doeth truth cometh to the light, that his deeds may be made manifest, that they are wrought in God.

xiv Able To Bear It   By Gertrude Grace Sanborn

Able To Bear It

By GERTRUDE GRACE SANBORN

The purpose of this book is to show forth God's faithfulness in making "a way to escape," according to His Word, and to help others who may be in similar hard places.

"There hath no temptation taken you but such as is common to man: but God is faithful, who will not suffer you to be tempted above that ye are able; but will with the temptation also make a way to escape, THAT YE MAY BE ABLE TO BEAR IT" (1 Corinthians 10:13).

Poems by Gertrude Grace Sanborn

BIBLE FOR TODAY PUBLISHERS
900 Park Avenue
Collingswood, New Jersey 08108

PSALMS 127:3

"Lo, children are an heritage of the LORD: and the fruit of the womb is his reward."

Able To Bear It — By Gertrude Grace Sanborn

To Beverly Grace Sanborn

I have a little treasure,
Most too dear to tell by pen;
She's my precious little "half-chick"[1]
And her years are nearly ten.

She cannot talk, nor understand,
She was born that way, you see;
And she's 'twined around this heart of mine,
Her poor infirmity.

The tears I've shed, and the black long nights,
The hopeless, endless fears,
The anguish of a mother's heart
For fruitless empty years.

I turned one day to His dear face,
I placed her in His care;
I do not dread the coming years,
Nor find the load still there.

For He sent this little treasure
Too dear for line or pen;
This precious little "half-chick"
Whose years are nearly ten.
(1944)

---

[1] Spanish Fable

PSALMS 77:3
"I remembered God,
and was troubled:
I complained,
and my spirit was over-whelmed."

1
Only A Fable

When I was a little girl I read the story of "The Little Half Chick" and was touched and grieved in behalf of the mother hen and her little abnormal chick. I was saddened as I read of the little hen who had waited and watched until all the eggs in her nest were hatched into perfect baby chicks--except one. And this one was only a half chick. It could only half stand, half see, and half peep, because it was only half there.

The poor mother hen was so bewildered because this baby was different from her other chicks. Yet he bravely tried hard to be a whole chick and play with his brothers and sisters. I wept for the poor little half chick who would always be just a part of what he should have been, and I thought of the poor mother hen who would always be bewildered at this strange thing. But I was comforted to know that it was only a fable.

I had nearly forgotten this little story until one day nearly 30 years ago there came into our home a dear little "half chick," and I became like the little mother hen who was bewildered and couldn't understand.

Able To Bear It By Gertrude Grace Sanborn

> **PSALMS 77:9**
> "Hath God forgotten to be gracious? hath he in anger shut up his tender mercies?"

2
The Doctor Said

My story begins when the family next door shared the whooping cough with us! I took our children to the doctor to see if there was anything he could do to prevent them from having a severe case of that serious and taxing disease.

When the doctor was treating Audrey, age four, he noticed that Beverly Grace, two and one-half years younger, ran aimlessly about his office, trying to take his instruments and tools from the cases and cabinets. He noticed also that though I tried to restrain and correct her, she did not seem to obey or be in the least impressed with my words. Looking at her, he said, "*I think this child has something wrong with her brain. Is there any insanity in your family?*"

His startling and unusual question, which seemed then a little amusing to me, was but the first clue to the verdict of the child specialist to whom we later took Beverly. We could not believe it. We were stunned and shocked at his verdict. Our child, our dear little golden-haired two-year-old, had sustained an injury to her brain during birth. There was no remedy, no cure, no hope. Our baby would *never* become a normal child.

Able To Bear It   By Gertrude Grace Sanborn

LUKE 4:18b

"... He hath sent me
to heal
the brokenhearted ..."

3
I Cried

All the long way home from the doctor's office, I cried. Oh, the hopelessness, the helplessness of my situation! My beautiful baby girl, never to be like other little girls, never to grow up into sweet maturity, never to be a blessing to me or a comfort, always to be a child in her mind--a stupid, peculiar child!

I was crushed by this awful thing. This stigma of an abnormal child was more than I could bear. I was angry at our family physician whom I held responsible for this tragedy. Why had he been so careless with me and my baby?

I wondered at God my Father's dealings with me. Wasn't I His dear child, and hadn't I given my children to Him to be used for His glory? Then why was I so sternly dealt with? The cry of my anguished heart was *"Why, oh why, has this terrible thing touched our lives?"*

Our Gems

Spirit of God, I give to Thee
These jewels in my arms.
I know that Thou wilt guard them
And keep them from all harms.

Spirit of God, I give to Thee
All care of treasures rare.
Just set them for Thy glory,
For radiance anywhere.

Bright gems in a golden setting,
Our children, set in Thy love,
The finest gift I can offer
To Thee, my Father above.

4
I Prayed

I thought as a Christian mother, having already walked through deep waters and trial, that I was prepared for anything. Our oldest daughter, Vonnie, had been stricken when three years of age and spent three years in the hospital, but God in His marvelous grace restored her to health and gave her back to us.

But this was different. This sorrow touched my pride and my spirit as well as my heart. This was indeed a "strange thing" and I just couldn't understand it.

I prayed with pleadings and supplications. I wept out my grief to the only One to whom I could go. I begged God to heal her and make her a normal child. I knew full well that He could, for He is God and there is nothing too hard for Him. I reminded Him of His promises in the Book regarding our prayers and afflictions. I prostrated my heart before Him and agonized in behalf of our little girl whom He had given us.

I remembered how happy I had been when I brought her home from the hospital and showed her to her two sisters. How I rejoiced from a thankful heart and with real joy that God in His great goodness had given me three children to rear for His glory and service. My cup was full and truly running over.

The Cost

Little did I know
The day I gave to Him my all,
The cost of such surrender,
Or the meaning of His call.

My plans, my thoughts, my talents,
My children, did I bring.
I laid them on the altar
For my Lord and heavenly King.

He accepted them from me,
For I gladly placed them there.
Then He began to use me
And the children that I bare.

Ah, not in place of honor,
Or high favor, or acclaim,
But He gently made us lowly,
Thus to magnify His Name.

5
I Became Weary

While the family slept, my nights were filled with worries and troubled thoughts regarding this problem, which seemed to have no solution. What of the long years that lay ahead? How would I manage as she grew older and larger and her mind stood still? What if I should die? Who would love this unlovely child enough to care for her? I could not find an answer.

Not only did she grieve me mentally and spiritually, but she was such a great and constant care that I became weary and exhausted in my body. Then, of course, there were the regular household duties which I performed without any outside assistance, and a husband and two normal children to care for and to serve.

"Oh, Lord," I thought and prayed, "if I could just run away from this thing, if I could hide myself somewhere until this dark cloud passes by. Is there no way out, no way to escape for me? Is there no release, ever? No help? Oh, my Father, this thing is too hard for me."

14 Able To Bear It   By Gertrude Grace Sanborn

The Lord, Our Banner

So tired, till I found His shadow
And sat down in His calm.

So sad, till I felt His compassion
On my soul as a healing balm.

So weak, till I saw o'er me His banner
And knew He was strong in the fray.

So homesick to go on to meet Him
So glad He is coming some day.

6
My Friends

Life has its way of going on, stopping for no man's losses or gains, leaving behind the tears and cares of yesterday and bringing new joys and tears and responsibilities. My friends were helpful, kind, and sympathetic. One dear friend occasionally cared for Beverly so that I could assist in church work, or could take a day's rest somewhere. The folk in our little church were all so understanding and tender. The pastor's wife especially was a blessing as she encouraged and comforted me on many hard days. Then there were the thrilling and instructive messages by the beloved pastor on the truth of the second coming of Christ. He was coming again, and for me! He might come today! I went home and read and reread the Scripture to my heart. I must not be ashamed at His coming!

Some friends, in trying to be helpful, suggested that I should take Beverly to a faith healer. Others in sincerity told me that I didn't pray in faith, or she would be healed. Still others thought that there might be sin in my heart so He would not hear. One dear one asked why God should punish a child for the sins of his parents or grandparents.

I began to understand about Job and his friends in a way that I never had done before. I looked into my heart. It was full of sin and pride. Perhaps my friends were right. Perhaps there was something in my life that was holding up God's answer and the healing. I "took out" my faith and examined it in the light of God's

Word and found that it was indeed a frail small thing. "Oh, Lord Jesus, what must I do? What is it that I have done or not done? I believe, help Thou mine unbelief, if that is what I need to make Beverly whole."

PSALMS 78:2-3

I will open my mouth in a parable: I will utter dark sayings of old: Which we have heard and known, and our fathers have told us.

7
The Pride of Life

As I began to memorize Scripture, a passage in 1 John 2 spoke to my heart. Before, it had been simply words on a page, but now it became indeed the Word of God, the Sword of the Spirit, piercing and searching. "... *All that is in the world, the lust of the flesh, and the lust of the eyes, and the pride of life, is not of the Father, but is of the world*" (1 John 2:15-16).

The pride of life, of the world? Did this mean that my pride was worldliness? My pride in having a spick-and-span home? My pride in accomplishment, that no task planned was ever left undone? My pride in my children, my beautiful children (Beverly was a pretty child and had a perfect body)? My hurt pride regarding Beverly? My stuffy self-evaluation? my pride of position in life-was this worldliness? I asked myself the cold question, *"Why was I grieving so over this strange trial?"* Beverly's condition caused her no discomfort. She was not intelligent enough to realize that she was abnormal. Why was I rebellious and worrying and fighting this thing which God had permitted?

Slowly, God's Word began to do its perfect work in my proud heart. Surely and certainly it brought conviction as to my state. I saw that keeping my home spotless left little time for devotion or Bible study, and that my love of order was merely pride of ability. I saw the heart of this lesson for me. Regarding Beverly, had I not said, "*Oh, Lord, why should this thing happen to me? Why am I chained to this problem and hindered from doing*

Able To Bear It — By Gertrude Grace Sanborn

what I want to do? Why did I have to have a child who was abnormal? This might happen to others, but why to me?"

I had always desired three lovely daughters. I could even see in my mind's eye how pretty they would look in later years, singing publicly for the Lord, being in places of leadership, witnessing, or perhaps even in special work in the church. Oh, bitter conviction! Oh, discerning Word! at worldliness I had drifted into or perhaps never risen above. Spiritual pride or natural pride was not of the Father, but of the world.

Grace

Hard is the pathway of training,
Stern is the way He may use
To take our dim eyes from earth things,
To make us His own will to choose.

How often our hands seem to cling to
The baubles and toys of this sphere!
But a wonderful, wise Overseer
Will give us of things far more dear.

He seats us in heavenly places,
Enfolds us around with His care,
Bestows us with gifts for His glory
That we may be used everywhere.

He lets us see failure in others,
Permits us to weep over loss,
Yet all of this while He is turning
Our hearts from this world to His cross.

8
He Cares For Me

I cannot explain the sweet peace that came to me with surrender. I meant it and my Lord knew I meant it. I wanted only His dear way, though I confess He lifted me up often when I drooped in spirit and body, and He closed my *murmuring mouth* in time of need by the manifold provision of His marvelous grace.

Gradually a new pattern, a way to escape, became evident, and clearly from Him. I wanted to please Him more than I wanted anything else in the world, even more than having Beverly healed. I ceased to pray for her healing and sought only strength for the day and for each duty and time for meditation in the precious Word of God.

Though I had a kind husband and thoughtful, helpful children, it seemed that I was so alone in this problem, by the very nature of it. Those most dear, though loving and compassionate, could not really enter into all that was involved, or quite understand my heart attitude or position. Often I felt that no one cared. The family, off to school and work and away from the tenseness and constancy of it, would come home refreshed and relieved, amazed that I was not bubbling and exuberant with life.

But somehow my loving heavenly Father helped me through all those weary, tiring days, and gave me strength for each duty as wife and mother. He cared for me, and I knew it. How this warming truth flowed over my heart as a balm! I learned to trust Him day by day and to leave tomorrow in His hands.

Able To Bear It   By Gertrude Grace Sanborn

God's Tomorrow

Take no thought for tomorrow,
For tomorrow is not in thy care.
Take no thought for tomorrow,
With its joy or its loss or its care.

The Father has given today
To live and to use and to see;
And has hidden in wonderful wisdom
Tomorrow from you and me.

He knows of its pain and its anguish
And helps us along tenderly,
Equipping by trials of the present
To stand in the new day to be.

9
Knowing The Doctrine

God gave me wonderful portions from the Word, which seemed, just for me alone. He supplied helps along the way. A little Christian paper that my husband brought home every week proved to be such a blessing. Whenever there was an opportunity, I rested while reading the *Gospel Herald*. When I ate lunch, I propped the paper before me so that I could learn from my favorite author and have spiritual and physical food. I used it for short devotions as soon as the girls and their daddy were off to work and school. It was so convenient to pick up and it was designed for just such a need as I had at the time. I used to cut out Scripture portions which were in large print and hang them over the kitchen sink so that I could memorize them as I worked. I recall the first one that I learned. It was Titus 2:11-14. I shall never forget how this portion stirred me to live "*soberly and righteously*" in my present world, and kept me looking up and away from myself.

A whole new world began to unfold to my eager heart while trusting in John 7:17, "*If any man will do his will, he shall know of the doctrine . . .* " I discovered many wonderful study books, and as God opened up to me this vast new field, He also opened up the eyes of my understanding. I knew little about theological books or their authors. I remember reading a fine book, drawn from the church library, written by Lewis Sperry Chafer. So ignorant was I that I asked the pastor who these three men were! But gradually with the assistance and counsel of my pastor, his dear wife, and also from the footnote references in the books themselves, I began to acquire and read the works of great men of

22 Able To Bear It   By Gertrude Grace Sanborn

God. I began in some measure to "*comprehend with all saints what is the breadth, and length, and depth, and height; And to know the love of Christ . . .*" and the mighty plan of God.

Using these books as helps, my Bible became my treasure and my stay. I was truly lifted above my circumstances and transported into the heavenlies. As I saw things with spiritual eyes, my cares grew strangely lightened and of less importance. I had found a way to escape (1 Corinthians 10:13). A gracious God supplied the means and my understanding husband permitted me to acquire a splendid reference library.

PSALMS 138:8
"The LORD will perfect that which concerneth me: thy mercy, O LORD, endureth for ever: forsake not the works of thine own hands."

Able To Bear It   By Gertrude Grace Sanborn

Deep in God's Word

Deep in God's Word there is hidden
Such wonders I gasp to behold;
The purpose of God and the mysteries
The Spirit of Truth does unfold.

Hidden behind words so common,
Yet plain to the heart that will look,
Are the treasures of Truth and His glory;
They are here in this wonderful Book.

Over and over and over again
I read, and the pages seem new.
I sing in my heart while I praise Him
And behold what the reading will do.

My mind is so eager to study,
My heart is so slow to believe,
But here on the page it is written,
And the Spirit leads me to receive.

How can I ever stop seeking,
The profit is greater each day;
And I find it is Christ I discover
As I meditate, listen, and pray.

Able To Bear It
By Gertrude Grace Sanborn

1 CORINTHIANS 10:13c

". . . God is faithful, who will not suffer you to be tempted above that ye are able; but will . . . also make a way to escape, that ye may be able to bear it."

10

A Way To Escape

Perhaps there are other ways for people to solve their problems and bear their burdens. Perhaps for those who have not Christ there is philosophy or similar reasoning. But for the Christian, Christ is the answer, for in Him are found all the treasures of wisdom and knowledge. As for me, I find no answer, no place of refuge, no solution, no escape but in the Word of God as I read it and lay hold of it. It is in this Book that I see my Lord, "touched" with the feeling of my infirmity, and I see His purpose, His power and His love for me.

Modern thinking tells us that to long for Heaven and the unseen things of eternity is to long for an escape from reality. In this they are partly correct. To read of Him, to see by faith His lovely face on the pages of that holy Book, to see that *Place* prepared for me by nail-pierced hands, and to read of my dear ones gone on to it, for me there is indeed release and escape from the force and presence of trials. But the reality is in Heaven, the shadow is here. Escape? Yes, it is escape. And with tears in my eyes, I flee to the Book and I cling to the Rock while I tremble.

What a wonder, that I may be transported by the vehicle of "God-breathed" words, out of the temporal and into the very eternal. These are the cities of refuge for me: the precious things (Bezer); fellowship and communion (Hebron); the strength of His shoulder (Shechem); the heights of witness (Ramah); the riches (Golan); and worship (Kadesh).[2] In the midst of Canaan I find He has provided a refuge for every need, and I shall, by His grace, dwell in "that city" (Joshua 20:6) until I stand in His presence.

PSALMS 138:2

"I will worship toward thy holy temple, and praise thy name for thy lovingkindness and for thy truth: for thou hast magnified thy word above all thy name."

---

[2] Cf. *Cruden's Concordance*, and F. W. *Grant's Numerical Bible* for these definitions.

Now for a Season

Only a moment,
Then hours forever;
Just for today,
Then years by His side.
Suffering a while,
Then called into Glory;
Now for a season,
Then, to abide.

Here, light affliction,
There, weight of glory.
Here, manifold trials,
There, found to His praise.
Here, songs in the night,
There, only morning.
Here, but the earnest,
There, joy all the days.

Earth but a tent,
Heaven a mansion.,
Clay but to crumble,
Silver shall stand.
Sands, always shifting,
The Rock, firm forever,
Long wilderness waiting,
Soon, reward from His hand.

Able To Bear It By Gertrude Grace Sanborn

PSALMS 73:25-26

"Whom have I in heaven but thee? and there is none upon earth that I desire beside thee. My flesh and my heart faileth: but God is the strength of my heart, and my portion for ever."

11
How Precious

When one has an abnormal child, the little progress that she makes along the way seems very important and gives great joy to those who love her. So it was that day when she first called me "Mommy." She was about ten years old. Many times, we mothers become harassed at the clamor of children's voices calling "Mother," but to me this was indeed a great day, to hear her little lips speak my name.

I think that when I shall stand in the presence of my Lord and Savior, one of the most wonderful things, next to hearing Him call my name, will be to hear my little Beverly Grace speak and say, "*I love you, Mother.*" During all these long years of caring for her and serving her, she has never indicated that she knew she was heart of my heart or flesh of my flesh.

Precious Problem

Dear little precious problem,
That God has given to me,
'Twined round my very being
Her sad deformity.

Gladly in love I serve her,
And all of her weakness bear,
Dear little precious problem
That God has put in my care.

Grace that He lets me have it,
Marvel He trusts me so,
Always He helps me share it
Because He loves me so.

Strange are His ways to show me
His way and His power and peace,
But perfect His manner and method
To bring forth a sure increase.

Dear are the daily duties
And tender each work of love
While I care for my precious problem
Because she is the one I love.

12
Shut Up To Him

As she became older, she required more care and supervision. She was no longer a little child. She was fast becoming a young lady, normal in all physical respects. More and more it was wise to remain at home with her. I became aware that God was keeping me home, and that any service which I might be permitted to do for Him would not be a public one. It seemed I was shut up to Him and to her.

How wise was God my Father's way, for after repeated efforts to fit Beverly into normal living, I would come home each time discouraged and exhausted. This was partly from the sheer effort of willing her to obey, and the strength expended in propelling her along. The stares of the curious hurt me so and their rudeness cut me to the heart. Thus it was I began to live shut up, as it were, from most normal activities in order to learn better the mind of the Lord and how He would have me care for her.

Each morning I studied His Word and claimed His promised provision of strength to do my many duties. "... *Seek ye first the kingdom of God, and his righteousness; and all these things shall be added unto you*" was what the Bible said. The "*all things*" I needed were strength, patience, and wisdom. Every day that I kept my part, He provided the "*all things.*"

Looking back, I now see how loving and wise was His plan and care for me. His way was "the escape," and I, who loved to be a leader, was being led. I who loved to sing to others was now the audience for the song of the Spirit. I, who aspired to teach, sat with greater privilege at the feet of the great Teacher, the Spirit of Truth Himself.

A new thing began to stir in my soul and I accepted it as being from the God of all grace, as one of the things which He added. I discovered that there was melody and poetry in my being, and that I could, by the simple medium of a pen, put down on paper the expressions and cries of my heart. These poems have helped some others and they have been a release and blessing to me. A few are included in this writing. Truly, many things were added to me as I was shut away, "a garden inclosed" (Song of Solomon 4:12; Lamentations 3:7).

LAMENTATIONS 3:7
"He hath hedged me about, that I cannot get out: he hath made my chain heavy."

Able To Bear It   By Gertrude Grace Sanborn

Learning

Blessed lonely desolations,
Blessed hour I found no friend,
Blessed day, when tears kept falling,
Blessed night that had no end.

For 'tis then, I found my refuge
As I fled to Jesus' feet.
There He held in sweet compassion,
There He all my grief did meet.

Had I never been so lonely,
Had I never needed grace,
I would ne'er have looked to Jesus,
Really seen His tender face.

So I thank Him for the journey
Through the valley and the test,
For I needed just that lesson
So I'd learn He knoweth best.

Genesis 41:52b

Able To Bear It
By Gertrude Grace Sanborn

> **1 JOHN 3:2**
>
> "Beloved, now are we the sons of God, and it doth not yet appear what we shall be: but we know that, when he shall appear, we shall be like him; for we shall see him as he is."

13
Recognition

Some may call it "*resignation*," but I call it "*recognition*"-- recognition of the sovereignty of God in all things. I no longer ask "*Why?*" "*for shall the thing formed say unto Him that formed it . . .*" "*Why?*" "*Hath not the potter power over the clay . . .* ? (Romans 9:21). Christians are urged to let go and let God have His wonderful way. But I say that whether we let go or not, God will have His wonderful way in our lives, because He is sovereign.

It is now more than ten years since God in His great wisdom took our beloved second daughter, Audrey, to be with Him at the age of twenty. At the completion of her senior year in high school, she was strangely and tragically stricken with the mysterious and dreaded Hodgkin's disease (cancer of the lymph glands). She lived two and a half years by God's grace through days of weakness and exhaustion, tears and heartbreak, but she came through the test and trial submissive to His will. I shall never forget at the end of her illness her words, "*Mother, I am asking the Lord to take me Home.*" These were the most wonderful, and yet heartbreaking words, I have ever heard. Beautiful because it meant that Heaven was Home to her, that she knew the Savior so intimately that she called being in His presence "*Home*." But heartbreaking, because it meant separation for me from my little girl. Yet these dear words of faith made me able to bear it.

Able To Bear It By Gertrude Grace Sanborn

Audrey

God gave to my arms a girl baby
So perfect and healthy and dear.
We nourished and cherished her daily
And were always protectingly near.

She grew to a beautiful maiden,
Quite lovely of face and of form.
She charmed all who saw with her manner
So honest and friendly and warm.

Then our Father from mansions of Glory
In wisdom that none can gainsay,
Took from my arms this dear treasure
And enclosed her in His one sad day.

November 1952   **Job 1:21**

Able To Bear It   By Gertrude Grace Sanborn

Her Empty Room
(1952)

I went up to her room one day
And looked in all her doors.
I opened up her cupboard
And peered into her stores.
I was so calm when I began
To sort and rearrange;
But as I touched her treasures,
My thoughts began to change.
The days gone by swept o'er me,
Before she went away.
I had to stop and leave that room
Until another day.

I went up to His house that day,
By means of fervent prayer;
I saw her there so lovely
Beside the golden stair.
Far better was the robe she wore
Than any cloth made here;
More lovely was reality
Than any dream held dear.
Oh Lord, just keep me looking
Up to that wondrous place
And when my heart grows lonely,
Turn there my eyes in grace.

But even in this trial, God, in His tenderness, turned our loss to His gain. During her illness, Audrey had written several lovely songs of praise, and these we were permitted to have printed and recorded. Several hundred of these recordings have been used

Able To Bear It   By Gertrude Grace Sanborn

of the Lord as a witness and a testimony of His care for those who trust Him. One of these songs is given here.

[If you wish, you may order a CD of Audrey Sanborn's songs by phoning 856-854-4452 or by writing Bible For Today, 900 Park Avenue, Collingswood, New Jersey 08108.]

ISAIAH 41:10

"Fear thou not; for I am with thee: be not dismayed; for I am thy God: I will strengthen thee; yea, I will help thee; yea, I will uphold thee with the right hand of my righteousness."

Able To Bear It By Gertrude Grace Sanborn

He Cares for Me

By Audrey June Sanborn
(1932-1952)

I must not fear, for my Lord is near
And He never slumbers nor sleeps.
He hears my cry, though I wonder why,
And my soul in His care He keeps.

Sad thoughts will cease, as He gives me peace
His grace is sufficient for me.
He saved my soul,
He can make me whole,
Compassionate Savior is He.

Dark hours are long, but I sing a song,
For He gives me songs in the night.
Though time goes slow,
He loves me I know
And some day He'll make all things right.

Life's road is long, but His arms are strong
And His strength is perfect in me.
He is my friend, on Him I depend.
Eternal Companion is He.

CHORUS
I am kept, within His care
There I find contentment.
I am one of His own,
He cares for me,
He cares for me.

Able To Bear It   By Gertrude Grace Sanborn

Some have expressed amazement that it was God's way to take a normal person and leave behind one such as Beverly, who was of no apparent value here. This grieved me, to hear such words, for my husband and my friends loved our Beverly Grace very dearly, and now that her sister had gone to be with the Lord, it seemed we loved her even more. How *very* precious she had become to us! We gave to her our particular love and devotion, and in a special sense she became our blessing.

---

2 CORINTHIANS 1:3
"Blessed be God, even the Father of our Lord Jesus Christ, the Father of mercies, and the God of all comfort . . ."

14
Comforted

A new problem presented itself when Audrey (two and a half years older than Beverly) went to be with the Lord, for her going shocked Beverly greatly. She missed her sister and all the little ministrations she had performed for her. It was hard for her to understand where Audrey was, and how it tore our hearts to see her go up to that empty room and look in vain. I yearned to be able to communicate to her from God's Word concerning the resurrection, and to share with her the marvelous peace by which God sustained us.

She lost weight and became very fearful lest we, too, would leave her. Though at best she had only a few abilities, she retrogressed several years and had to be taught again and again. In some respects she was never able to pick up the thread of understanding and she forgot entirely many little helpful habits which were her usual routine.

You may well imagine that this was very taxing and required much patience and wisdom which I can truly testify came only from my kind Father. Looking back now at that difficult time, when my heart was saddened and bereaved, I can but bow before His matchless wisdom as I realize that just at the right time He permitted these extra cares so that I would not be overwhelmed by my grief.

I shall never forget the understanding sympathy and practical love of my dear mother, who helped me during those **very hard days.** She often cared for Beverly so that I could slip away for a respite from her constant crying. My mother understood my heart in those sad days, for she had watched her own son suffer and depart this life at a young age. I thought that I understood at that time, but I now have learned that I stood outside the comprehension of her loss.

PSALMS 57:1

"Be merciful unto me, O God, be merciful unto me: for my soul trusteth in thee: yea, in the shadow of thy wings will I make my refuge, until these calamities be overpast."

Able To Bear It   By Gertrude Grace Sanborn

Understanding
To My Mother

I thought I understood
When your dear one went away.
I stood by you and grieved with you
And wiped your tears away.

But came to me such sorrow
When my dear one said, "Goodbye"
I really understand your grief,
Since such a loss have I.

I am comforted when I think of the Lord Jesus Christ's soon coming and I wait, not only because it will solve my problem, but because I long to see His face. Each day I see God's hand in preparing opportunities to speak a word for Him. People come to me, with whom I would otherwise have no contact, because they are moved to speak about Beverly's condition. How can I help but praise Him when He sets before me such doors of utterance? In many places and in strange circumstances I am privileged to tell of His love for me and His love for them. Sometimes I talk to a person at the store, or at the shop where I buy her clothes, or when I buy a few supplies at the grocery store. Sometimes as I sit in the car with her, people stop and talk. It is indeed like the following allegory of the wise and loving king:

Able To Bear It   By Gertrude Grace Sanborn

PSALMS 59:16-17

"But I will sing of thy power; yea, I will sing aloud of thy mercy in the morning: for thou hast been my defence and refuge in the day of my trouble. Unto thee, O my strength, will I sing: for God is my defence, and the God of my mercy."

Able To Bear It   By Gertrude Grace Sanborn

Bearing and Leaning
(An allegory of a wise and loving king)

There was once a loving and wise king who had great riches which he wished to share with the people of his kingdom. He sent his servants out into the highways and the byways to tell this wonderful story of his gift of love.

There were many servants who went forth to tell the good news, but not many people were willing to stop long enough to hear it. The wise king knew that it would be so, and had prepared a plan which would cause the people to stop and listen.

It seemed to many to be a strange and unusual plan, for the king had selected some of his special servants and upon them placed heavy burdens.

Though the burdens were different for each servant, they were all heavy, and some were very, very heavy. Before the king sent them forth to tell of his great gift, he gave them each a strong staff to lean upon as they walked.

Thus, the servants went forth, bearing their burdens, leaning upon the staff as they walked. Up the highways and into the valleys they went, and everywhere people stopped and in genuine sympathy and interest offered to help. They always asked about the burden; what kind it was and if it was very heavy, and who placed it there and why. They noticed the

Able To Bear It   By Gertrude Grace Sanborn

strong staff and observed how the servants had to lean upon it as they walked. The special servants walked on and on, through many days, and talked to many people, and while answering questions about the burden, told about the great king and his gift of love.

Some days the servants became very weary, and longed to lay aside their burdens. Some days the hills were very steep and some nights the way was lonely and drear. The king called to them one day and spoke to them regarding their loads. But after listening to his voice and talking face to face with him, not one was willing to go forth without his burden. Not even those who carried very, very heavy burdens. They knew that it was because of their loads people stopped and talked to them and thus heard the story. They also knew that they had walked so long, leaning upon the staff, that they could no longer walk without leaning.

So, dear servant of God, burden-laden and weary, keep plodding on, trusting His Word, knowing that it is for His excellent name's sake and to the salvation of souls. Let us serve daily our wise and sovereign Lord, who has permitted us to bear a burden that we might be more profitable servants.

There will be a day soon when He will call us aside, and then the dear hands that placed the trials will remove them. Until that day, let us press on, bearing our burden, leaning upon the staff, the Word of God.

> *"Set me as a seal upon thine heart, as a seal upon thine arm: for love is*

strong as death; jealousy is cruel as the grave: the coals thereof are coals of fire, which hath a most vehement flame." (Song of Solomon 8:6)

I am constantly amazed that He has stooped to save me from my sin, that He has in grace chosen me and permitted me to serve Him with a burden. Though I do not ask "Why?" I do ask "When?" For the truth of His soon coming brings me peace. It is the hope that sustains me when my heart and body falter. It is the beacon before me when I cannot see the light. It is the balm for my bruised soul when I feel that no one cares. It is truly the "blessed hope," for it is the day when He will come and make all things perfect.

For years I believed that it was selfish to long for His return so that all problems would be solved. There were yet so many who were not ready. But I have since learned that He has recorded this truth in His wonderful Book for us to believe, and that the whole Scripture breathes out comfort and encouragement to us all, with the hope of that glad day. Furthermore, we are urged to comfort one another with these words.

Able To Bear It — By Gertrude Grace Sanborn

PSALMS 18:2

"The LORD is my rock, and my fortress, and my deliverer; my God, my strength, in whom I will trust; my buckler, and the horn of my salvation, and my high tower."

15
Able To Bear It

The years are now very many since that day when God my Father allowed this hard thing to come upon my life, and bid me place my weak hand in His. Step by step and tear by tear He has led me from seeming loss to acknowledged gain, to the very place of service and witness which He has foreordained for me, His very own child. Never for one moment has my Lord left me to ponder my cares alone, but is always there faithfully standing "*behind our wall*" and "*shewing Himself through the lattice*" (Song of Solomon 2:9), faithful in every lesson and test to provide a way to escape that I may be able to bear it.

These have been years of peculiar trials and proving. I can look back now and trace the hand of my Heavenly Father leading, directing and restraining as He bids me walk *through* the valleys and into the shadows, for His dear name's sake.

How well I remember when this thing *was first laid on me*, how I repeatedly sought to give it back to Him and to be released. I thought that if we asked in faith He would remove the burden. I did not know, but since have learned, that when God gives or permits trials and testings, He does so for a purpose, His great purpose; and He intends us to live for Him, and to bear fruit unto Him in spite of the burdens and in *the midst of* the trials.

PROVERBS 3:5-6

"Trust in the LORD with all thine heart; and lean not unto thine own understanding. In all thy ways acknowledge him, and he shall direct thy paths."

Able To Bear It   By Gertrude Grace Sanborn

A Prayer

Help me to trust Thee
For all of my days.
Teach me, my Father
To rest in Thy ways.
Thou who hast formed me
And planned all my years,
Art greater than trials,
Disappointments or tears.

I know that the song writer has told us to take our burdens to the Lord and leave them there. It is a sweet and encouraging thought. However, we have the Scripture in 1 Corinthians 10:13 which speaks of His provision that we may be *able to* bear our burdens. Our God is faithful, for when He permits a trial He at the same time makes a way to escape that we can and may, as submissive Christians, bear that experience.

That He cares for us makes us willing to bear it; and that He sustains us makes us *"able to bear it."* Perhaps that is what is meant by that wonderful promise of Psalm 55:22, *"Cast thy burden upon the LORD, and he shall sustain thee,"* i.e., with thy burden.

And who of us has not fled to that holy rest promised us in Matthew 11:28-30, that marvelous invitation of grace that we, in our weakness, may rest upon omnipotence *and* learn of Him. His promises are as faithful as He Himself. He has promised perfect peace to those who will fix their minds on Him; grace at the very time of need; songs in the longest night; and spiritual melodies in the hearts. At the end of the hard day, we who trust His Word find that our day has been a day with Him during which

Able To Bear It — By Gertrude Grace Sanborn

we have beheld His great faithfulness. He has not "*suffered us to be tempted above that which we are able.*"

I am thankful to the Lord for many things: for my health and for the health of my husband; for perfect restoration of Vonnie, our eldest daughter, who with her pastor-husband encouraged me to share this story; and also for the blessing of five dear grandchildren. And now after these many years, Beverly is an even greater care and responsibility; yet He keeps me sustained by the marvelous provision of His Word. I am able to go from faith to faith because we go together. Actually He lifts me up in His arms of strength, while I hold her up in my arms of flesh. She leans her infirmity against me, the while I lean upon Him; thus trusting Him for all things I am "*able to bear it.*"

Many things have been written about suffering and burden bearing, and much can still be written, yet most of that which has been said will leave unanswered the cry of those dear saints of God who quietly and without rebellion ask, "*Why, Lord?*" and "*How, Lord?*"

Romans 8:18

"For I reckon that the sufferings of this present time are not worthy to be compared with the glory which shall be revealed in us."

Able To Bear It   By Gertrude Grace Sanborn

Since I Learned To Trust Him
By Audrey June Sanborn
(1932–1952)

Since I learned to love and trust the Saviour,
Learned to cast on Him my every care,
Followed when He led in deepest waters,
I have learned to live with Him in prayer.

Pressing care and weakness may possess me,
Pain and languor hold me in their sway,
Strange it is, though this may be my portion,
I have learned I can rejoice today.

Patiently He speaks and says He loves me,
Slowly I've responded to His Word,
Now it matters not, just that He leads me,
For I've learned to wait and trust the Lord

CHORUS
He has now become so very precious
He has now become so very dear
And I feel I know Him better
Since I have learned to trust Him here.

Able To Bear It By Gertrude Grace Sanborn

Why?

Torn in my heart still,
As I gaze in the face
Of my poor little child
Named Beverly Grace.

So void of maturity,
Wisdom or thought.
Never to learn,
And never be taught.

Years now are added,
The days have fled by,
And though not in rebellion
I still wonder, "Why?"

This author does not claim any ability, but has claimed God's promise to make a way to escape so as to be able to bear any burden which God in His purpose permits us to carry. It is with the hope of helping others to also find the way to escape that this has been written. It is but a simple narration of a great provision, and an encouragement to serve Him with our burden and for the discernment to recognize and accept His way to escape. I offer this testimony--urging that we believe God's Word, that whatever comes to our lives by His permission or direction will be worked together for our good, that we, being able to bear it, may be sooner conformed to His image.

I recall that lovely portion in the Song of Solomon, chapter 8, verse 5: "*Who is this that cometh up from the wilderness, leaning upon the arm of her beloved?*" And reverently

Able To Bear It   By Gertrude Grace Sanborn

I respond in answer, "Lord, it is I." Drawing upon such strength, we must conclude with the Apostle Paul, that though we be chastened we are not killed, and though sorrowful we are able to rejoice, and though we may be poor, we may make many rich (2 Corinthians 6:9-10).

Have we not been assured by His Word that He is able to save us, and able to keep us? And does it not also say that He is *able* to present us blameless and faultless? Shall we not, then, trust this same clear Word, which says that He will make a way to escape, *"that we may be able to bear it?"*

So while we wait for His coming, let us take that provided escape, the way of the Book, the way of surrender, the way of faith, and be "*Strengthened with all might, according to his glorious power, unto all patience and long-suffering with joyfulness*" (Colossians 1:11).

Victory

Some days I'm tired and weary
And clouds obscure His face,
But today His Word has shown me
That there is a resting place.

So now my heart is singing
And the world is fair to me,
For Jesus by His Spirit
Has given victory.

Able To Bear It   By Gertrude Grace Sanborn

Appendix
By Yvonne Sanborn Waite
(Mrs. Sanborn's oldest daughter)

It was while a friend and I were organizing my Mother's library that I discovered a book. It was a devotional book of comfort that she read. It was given to her by a friend. I looked. I read. I cried.

Soon, the devotional thoughts found within the pages of this book, moved my heart. It was then, I glanced at the back of the book, and discovered several poems written by my Mother. I don't think I had ever seen them. I was moved. Words cannot tell how touched I was. These poems talked of Gertrude Sanborn's emotions when my sister, Audrey June Sanborn, died. Some were written on the very day she died, at age 20, in November of 1952. There was one about my sister, Beverly Grace, also, who was born brain-damaged. She died in her 60's.

How I wished I had found these poems earlier. Previously, my husband and I had published over 400 of Mother's poems in a book called *With Tears In My Heart*. Perhaps you also have it in your possession.

It was as we were working on *Able To Bear It* that I realized I could put these precious, newly discovered poems in this very book for you to read. May God bless your heart as He has mine through these newly discovered words. They are so fresh. They are so piercing. They are so truthful.

Able To Bear It   By Gertrude Grace Sanborn

KEEP ME LOOKING UP

O, Lord, just keep me looking
Up to that lovely Place.
And when my heart grows lonely here,
Turn there, mine eyes, in grace.

Able To Bear It By Gertrude Grace Sanborn

THE THIEF
November 30, 1952
The date of Audrey's death

There came to my life a cruel stranger
Who broke into the vault of my heart,
And stole from my deep inner chamber
A jewel that was, of me, a part.

Ignoring my plans and my crying,
He ruthlessly took her away
And left me bereft of my treasure,
And saddened for all of my day.

THANK YOU, LORD
Answer to prayer regarding Beverly
March, 1954

Thank you, Lord, for answered prayer.
Amazing is Thy grace,
To spare my further grief and deep distress.

Amazing, too, Thy method,
And the means Thou dost provide.
The One employed to save my helplessness.

Thank you, Lord, I'm encouraged more to trust,
To cast it all on Thee, if other trials come.

The way Thou workest out my problems
Brings thanks and praise to Thee, O Wisest One

LORD, I'M GLAD
On a Florida trp
March 2, 1954

Lord, I'm glad that I can come to Thee
With my every trial and care.
For no One else does enter in
Or can my burden bear.

How glad am I, that Thou, in grace,
Dost see my weariness.
For others think it's failure
When I weep in weak distress.

O keep mine eyes turned Godward
Away from self and pride,
And speed the day when the trumpet
Shall call me to Thy side.

I WONDER WHAT IT IS
In route to Florida
March 2, 1954

I wonder what it is
That my Father sees in me
That causes Him to lay the rod
With such consistency.

I wonder what He knows or thinks
When He sees my bent to sin.
Does He see that I would fail Him
If there were no chastening?

My heart is bowed in reverence
While my life is filled with tears.
For I feel His Great Omniscience
In my trials throughout the years.

I ALONE
June 27, 1954

She is gone.
And, of those who wept and missed her,
I alone remain.
They have found another love,
Another friend to meet their loss.
I alone can find no substitute,
No one to take her place.
I alone remain.
I am her mother.

SO LONG
1954

Never to hear her speak again
Or call me *Mother*.

Never to hear her sing a lovely song.
Gone is her young and vital presence.

Away–She'll be away
For, Oh, so long.

JUST A SHORT TIME
1954

Just a short time,
And we'll be Home with Jesus.
Just a little while,
And then we'll see His face.
Just a few more tears,
Then glad release will greet us.
Just a few more steps
In life's long, weary race.
Just a short time!

Able To Bear It   By Gertrude Grace Sanborn

Index of Words and Phrases

(2 Corinthians 6:9-10) 55
1 Corinthians 10:13 22
1 Corinthians 10:13 .... vi, ix, 1, 24, 51
1 John 2 17
1 John 2:15-16 17
1 JOHN 3:2 34
1932-1952 39
1944 3
1952 .... 36, 37, 39, 53, 57, 59
1954 60-65
2 CORINTHIANS 1:3 40
30 years ago 5
A Prayer .... xii, 51
a respite from her 42
a way to escape .... vi, xi, 1, 19, 22, 24, 25, 49, 51, 54, 55
Able To Bear It . 1, i, vi-ix, xii, 1, 24, 35, 49, 51, 52, 54, 55, 57
able to bear our burdens 51
abnormal chick 5
abnormal child 9, 29
abnormal. 17
afflictions 11
age of twenty .... viii, 35
allegory of a wise and loving king 45
Audrey .... v, viii, ix, xii, 7, 35-39, 41, 53, 57
Audrey June Sanborn .... ix, 39, 53, 57
Audrey Sanborn's songs 38
Audrey, dear girl v
Audrey's death 59
author .... iv, v, xi, 21, 54
baby girl 9
balm 14, 19, 47

beacon before me 47
Bearing and Leaning 45
bearing our burden 46
beautiful 9, 17, 35, 36
beautiful baby girl 9
beautiful maiden 36
became very fearful 41
begged God 11
Beverly .... v, xi, 3, 7, 15-17, 19, 29, 31, 40-42, 52, 54, 57, 60
Beverly Grace .... xi, 3, 7, 29, 40, 54, 57
Beverly Grace Sanborn .... xi, 3
BFT Phone: 856-854-4452 iii
BFT@BibleForToday.org iii
Bible .... 1, i, iii, vii, xii, 1, 17, 22, 26, 31, 38
Bible For Today Baptist Church iii
BIBLE FOR TODAY MINISTRIES vii
BIBLE FOR TODAY PUBLISHERS 1-1
Bible study 17
birth 7
blessed hope 47
Blessed lonely desolations 33
Book .... vii-ix, xi, 1, 11, 21, 23, 25, 47, 55, 57
born that way 3
brain 7, 57
burdens .... viii, 25, 45, 46, 49, 51
cancer .... viii, 35
cancer of the lymph glands 35
careless 9
Cast thy burden upon the LORD 51
Chafer 21
chastening 62
child in her mind 9
child specialist 7
Christ .... viii, ix, 15, 22, 23, 25, 40

Christ is the answer	viii, 25
Christian	viii, 11, 21, 25
Christian mother	11
Christian paper	21
Church Phone: 856-854-4747	iii
cities of refuge	25
claimed His promised provision	31
Clay but to crumble	27
Collingswood	1, i, iii, 1, 38
Collingswood, New Jersey	1, i, iii, 1, 38
Colossians 1:11	55
comfort one another	47
Comforted	vii, xii, 5, 15, 41, 43
coming again	15
Compassionate Savior	39
comprehension	42
consistency	62
consolation	vii
constant care	vii, 13
constant crying	42
Cover Design	iii
cried	xi, 9, 57
cries of my heart	32
cruel stranger	59
crushed	9
dark cloud	13
Dark hours are long	39
daughter	v, viii, 11, 35, 52, 57
dear friend	15
Deep in God's Word	23
deep waters	11
deepest waters	53
deformities	viii
despair	viii, ix

devotion	17, 40, 57
diagnosis	ix
Disappointments or tears	51
discomfort	17
discouraged and exhausted	31
Doctor	xi, 7
doctor's office	9
doctrine	xi, 21
doors of utterance	43
Dr. D. A. Waite	vii
dreadful diagnosis	ix
during birth	7
Earth but a tent	27
eldest daughter	52
encouragement	47, 54
escape	vi-viii, xi, 1, 13, 19, 22, 24, 25, 31, 49, 51, 54, 55
Eternal Companion is He	39
eternity	25
exhaustion	35
expressions	32
e-mail	iii
Fable	xi, 3, 5
faith healer	15
Far better was the robe she wore	37
Father	viii-10, 13, 17-20, 36, 40, 41, 49, 51, 62
fax: 856-854-2464	iii
fellowship and communion	25
fervent prayer	37
five dear grandchildren	52
Foreword	vii, xi
friendly and warm	36
Gems	xi, 10
Genesis 41:52b	33
Gertrude	1, i, iv, vii-ix, 1, 57

Able To Bear It   By Gertrude Grace Sanborn

Gertrude Grace Sanborn . . . . 1, i, iv, ix, 1
Gertrude Sanborn viii
girl baby 36
Glory 9-11, 18, 23, 27, 36, 52
go up to that empty room 41
God had permitted 17
God has allowed v
God has given each GIFT (child) v
God my Father 49
God my Father's dealings with me 9
God was keeping me home 31
God's faithfulness 1
God's hand 43
God's Tomorrow 20
God's Word 17, 23, 41, 54
God-breathed 25
God's Book--the Bible vii
God's hand viii
God's Words viii
Gospel Herald 21
Grace .. 1, i, iv, v, ix, xi, 1, 3, 7, 11, 18, 19, 26, 29, 30, 32, 33,
                 35, 37, 39, 40, 47, 51, 54, 57, 58, 60, 61
gracious God 22
great provision 54
great Teacher 32
grieve me 13
grieving . . . . viii, 17
half chick 5
half-chick 3
Has given victory 55
He all my grief did meet 33
He Cares for Me . . . . xi, xii, 19, 39
He gives me peace 39
He gives me songs in the night 39

He has now become so very precious 53
He hears my cry 39
He is coming some day 14
He is my friend 39
He is sovereign 35
He knoweth best 33
He loves me I know 39
healed 15, 19
healing 14, 15, 19
healing balm 14
health 11, 52
heartbreaking words 35
Heaven 25, 27, 28, 35
Heaven a mansion 27
Heaven was Home 35
heavenly Father .... viii, 19, 49
heavenly King 12
heavenly places 18
heavy burdens 45, 46
Help me to trust Thee 51
helping others 54
helplessness 9, 60
Her Empty Room .... xii, 37
her going shocked Beverly greatly 41
her little girl viii
His arms are strong 39
His arms of strength 52
His calm 14
His compassion 14
His cross 18
His grace is sufficient for me 39
His great faithfulness 52
His hands 19
His love for me .... ix, 25, 43

His matchless wisdom 41
His own will 18
His promises 11, 51
His return 47
His shadow 14
His tenderness 37
His way to escape 54
His wonderful Book 47
His Word 1, 31, 46, 51-53, 55
Hodgkin's disease .... viii, 35
holy Book 25
holy rest 51
Home 5, 9, 11, 15, 17, 19, 21, 31, 35, 65
Home with Jesus 65
homesick 14
hope .... vii, viii, 7, 47, 54
hopelessness 9
How Precious .... xi, 29
I ALONE .... xii, 63
I alone remain 63
I am asking the Lord to take me Home 35
I am kept, within His care 39
I am one of His own 39
I Became Weary .... xi, 13
I can rejoice today 53
I Cried .... xi, 9, 57
I had to stop and leave that room 37
I have learned to submit v
I long to see His face 43
I love you, Mother 29
I must not fear 39
I Prayed .... xi, 11
I sing a song 39
I still wonder, "Why?" 54

I touched her treasures 37
I WONDER WHAT IT IS . . . . xii, 62
illness . . . . viii, 35, 37
illnesses viii
incurable cancer viii
Index of Words and Phrases . . . . xii, 67
infirmity . . . . ix, 3, 25, 52
injury to her brain 7
insanity 7
ISAIAH 41:10 38
jewels 10
Job 1:21 36
Job and his friends 15
John 3:16-21 . . . . xi, xiii
John 7:17 21
June 27, 1954 63
JUST A SHORT TIME . . . . xii, 65
KEEP ME LOOKING UP . . . . xii, 58
keeping my home spotless 17
King James Bible . . . . iii, xii
know of the doctrine 21
Knowing The Doctrine . . . . xi, 21
Lamentations 3:7 32
lay the rod 62
leaning upon the staff 45, 46
Learning . . . . xi, xii, 33
leave behind 40
Lewis Sperry Chafer 21
Life has its way of going on 15
light affliction 27
little girl . . . . viii, 5, 11, 35
Little Half Chick 5
little treasure 3
long for His return 47

long nights	3
look in vain	41
looked to Jesus	33
Lord	v, vii-ix, xi, xii, 2, 12-14, 16-19, 22, 25, 29, 31, 35, 37-41, 43, 46, 48-53, 55, 58, 60, 61
Lord Jesus Christ	ix, 40
LORD, I'M GLAD	xii, 61
love of order	17
lovely of face	36
lovely Place	58
lovely songs of praise	37
LUKE 4:18b	8
magnify His Name	12
make a way to escape	vi, 1, 24, 54, 55
manifold trials	27
March 2, 1954	61, 62
March, 1954	60
Matthew 11:28-30	51
maturity	9, 54
meditate	23
melody	32
memorize Scripture	17
mighty plan of God	22
Mommy	29
mother	v, vii-ix, 5, 11, 19, 29, 35, 42, 43, 57, 63, 64
mother hen	5
mother's testimony	vii
Mrs. D. A. Waite	ix
Mrs. R. O. Sanborn	iv
murmuring mouth	19
my dear mother	42
my father	ix, 10, 13, 49, 51, 62
My Friends	xi, 15

my heart .. 11, 15, 17, 19, 23, 28, 29, 32, 37, 41, 42, 47, 54, 55, 57-59, 62
my heart is singing 55
my heart was saddened and bereaved 41
my kind Father 41
my mother .... vii, 42, 43, 57
my mother's testimony vii
my pride 11, 17
my refuge 33, 42
my spirit 4, 11
my stay 22
my treasure 22, 59
my weak hand in His 49
nail-pierced hands 25
needed grace 33
night that had no end 33
no apparent value 40
no friend 33
no thought 20
no way to escape 13
normal child 7, 9, 11, 29
normal person 40
not be ashamed at His coming 15
November 1952 36
November 30, 1952 59
Now for a Season .... xi, 27
Oh, Lord 13, 16, 17
oldest daughter 11, 57
omnipotence 51
on Him I depend 39
Only A Fable .... xi, 5
opportunities to speak 43
Orders: 1-800-John 10:9 iii
Our Gems .... xi, 10

Pain and languor	53
particular love and devotion	40
Pastor D. A. Waite	iii
pastor's wife	15
pastor-husband	52
patience	vii, 31, 41, 55
peculiar child	9
people stop and talk	43
permits trials and testings	49
Place prepared	25
plans	12, 59
pleadings	11
poems	ix, 1, 32, 57
Poems by Gertrude Grace Sanborn	1
poetry	32
pray	15, 19, 23
precious Word of God	19
Preface by the Author	v, xi
Pressing care and weakness	53
pretty child	17
pride	xi, 11, 15, 17, 18
pride of ability	17
pride of life	xi, 17
problem	xi, 13, 17, 19, 30, 41, 43
problems	viii, 25, 47, 60
prostrated my heart	11
proud heart	17
PROVERBS 3:5-6	50
Psalm 31:15	viii
Psalm 55:22	51
PSALMS 127:3	2
PSALMS 138:2	26
PSALMS 18:2	48
PSALMS 57:1	42

PSALMS 59:16-17	44
PSALMS 73:25-26	28
PSALMS 77:3	4
PSALMS 77:9	6
PSALMS 78:2-3	16
purpose of this book	xi, 1
R. O. Sanborn	iv, ix
rebellious	17
Recognition	xi, 35
recorded	37, 47
reference library	22
REGULAR BAPTIST PRESS	i, vii
release and blessing to me	32
resignation	35
rest in Thy ways	51
resting place	55
Romans 9:21	35
sad	14, 30, 36, 39, 42
Sad thoughts will cease	39
Sanborn	1, i, iv, v, viii, ix, xi, 1, 3, 39, 53, 57
Sands, always shifting	27
Savior	29, 35, 39
Scripture	15, 17, 21, 47, 51
second coming of Christ	15
second daughter, Audrey	35
seeming loss to acknowledged gain	49
seen His tender face	33
self-evaluation	17
share this story	52
she had watched her own son suffer	42
She is gone	63
She lost weight	41
She missed her sister	41
she retrogressed several years	41

Shut Up To Him .... xi, 31
sin in my heart 15
Since I Learned To Trust Him .... xii, 53
so lonely 33
SO LONG .... xii, 46, 64
soberly and righteously 21
solace and hope vii
Song of Solomon 32, 47, 49, 54
Song of Solomon 2:9 49
Song of Solomon 4:12 32
Song of Solomon 8:5 47
songs in the longest night 51
songs in the night 27, 39
sorrows .... v, viii, ix
sovereignty of God 35
spick-and-span home 17
Spirit of God 10
Spirit of Truth 23, 32
spiritual melodies in the hearts 51
stares .... vii, viii, 31
stares of the curious 31
Stern 18
strange thing 5, 11
Strengthened with all might 55
stricken 11, 35
strong staff 45, 46
studied His Word 31
study 17, 21, 23
stupid 9
submissive Christians 51
such a loss have I 43
suffering 27, 52, 55
Suffering a while 27
supervision 31

supplications 11
sweet compassion 33
Sword of the Spirit 17
sympathetic 15
Table of Contents xi
take a normal person 40
talents 12
tears and heartbreak 35
tears kept falling 33
temptation . . . . vi, 1
tempted above that which we are able 52
ten years old 29
tenseness 19
THANK YOU, LORD . . . . xii, 60
THE BIBLE FOR TODAY PRESS iii
The Cost . . . . xi, 12
The Doctor Said . . . . xi, 7
the escape 31
THE GOD OF ALL GRACE . . . . v, 32
The Lord, Our Banner . . . . xi, 14
The Pride of Life . . . . xi, 17
The Rock, firm forever 27
THE THIEF . . . . xii, 59
the valley and the test 33
theological books 21
there is Beverly v
thoughts 12, 13, 37, 39, 57
three children 11
three lovely daughters 18
three years in the hospital 11
three years of age 11
tired and weary 55
tiring days 19
Titus 2:11-14 21

To My Mother 43
tomorrow . . . . xi, 19, 20
Took from my arms this dear treasure 36
Torn in my heart 54
tragedy 9
training 18
treasures of Truth 23
trial . . . . v, 11, 17, 35, 37, 51, 61
trials and testings 49
troubled thoughts 13
Turn there my eyes in grace 37
two sisters 11
two-year-old 7
unbelief . . . . viii, ix, 16
Understanding . . . . xii, 15, 21, 22, 41-43, 50
understanding sympathy 42
unlovely child 13
unusualness viii
vault of my heart 59
very taxing 41
Victory . . . . vii, xii, 55
Vonnie 11, 52
Waite . . . . iii, v, vii, ix, 57
walk through the valleys 49
way to escape . . . . . . vi, xi, 1, 13, 19, 22, 24, 25, 49, 51, 54, 55
weak, ... 14
Website: www.BibleForToday.org iii
wept 5, 11, 63
whole chick 5
whooping cough 7
Why . . . . viii, xii, 9, 15, 17, 18, 35, 39, 45, 47, 52, 54
Why? . . . . xii, 35, 47, 54
wife and mother 19
wiped your tears away 43

wisdom .... vii, viii, 20, 25, 31, 35, 36, 41, 54
wise and loving king 43, 45
wise king 45
wise Overseer 18
Wisest One 60
Word of God .... viii, 17, 19, 25, 46
Words of God .... viii, ix
worries 13
worrying 17
wrong with her brain 7
young lady 31
Yvonne .... v, ix, 57
Yvonne Sanborn Waite .... v, ix, 57

Order Blank (p. 1)

Name:_____

Address:_____

City & State:_____ Zip:_____

Credit Card #:_____ Expires:_____

Latest Books

[ ] Send *Able To Bear It* by Gertrude G. Sanborn (106 pages Perfect bound $14.00 + $7.00 S&H)

[ ] Send *Gnosticism: The Doctrinal Foundation of the New Bible Versions* (213 pp. Perfect Bound ($20.00 + $8.00 S&H)

[ ] Send *Biblical Separation* By Dr. D. A. Waite (132 pp., Perfect Bound $14.00 + $7.00 S&H)

[ ] Send *Modern Version Failures* By Charles Kriessman (152 pp., Perfect bound $14.00 + $7.00 S&H)

[ ] Send *The Sixth 200 Questions Answered* By Dr. D. A. Waite (188 pp. perfect bound $15.00 + $7.00 S&H)

[ ] Send *The Fifth 200 Questions Answered* By Dr. D. A. Waite (150 pp. perfect bound $15.00 + $7.00 S&H)

[ ] Send *The Fourth 200 Questions Answered* By Dr. D. A. Waite (168 pp. perfect bound $15.00 + $7.00 S&H)

[ ] Send *The Third 200 Questions Answered* By Dr. D. A. Waite (180 pp. perfect bound $15.00 + $7.00 S&H)

[ ] Send *The Second 200 Questions Answered* By Dr. D. A. Waite (178 pp. perfect bound $15.00 + $7.00 S&H)

[ ] Send *The First 200 Questions Answered* By Dr. D. A. Waite (184 pp. perfect bound $12.00 + $7.00 S&H)

[ ] Send *A Critical Answer to James Price's King James Only-ism* By Pastor D. A. Waite, 184pp, perfect bound ($11+$7 S&H)

[ ] Send *The KJB's Superior Hebrew & Greek Words* by Pastor D. A. Waite, 104 pp., perfect bound ($10+$7 S&H)

Send or Call Orders to:
THE BIBLE FOR TODAY
900 Park Ave., Collingswood, NJ 08108
Phone: 856-854-4452; FAX:--2464; Orders: 1-800 JOHN 10:9

Order Blank (p. 2)

Name:_____

Address:_____

City & State:_____Zip:_____

Credit Card #:_____Expires:_____

[ ] Send *Soulwinning's Versions-Perversions* by Pastor D. A. Waite, booklet, 28 pp. ($6+$5 S&H) fully indexed

[ ] Send *2 Timothy--Preaching Verse by Verse*, by Pastor D. A. Waite, 250 pages, perfect bound ($11+$7 S&H) indexed.

[ ] Send *A Critical Answer to God's Word Preserved* by Pastor D. A. Waite, 192 pp. perfect bound ($11.00+$7.00 S&H)

[ ] Send *Daily Bible Blessings* By Yvonne Waite ($20+$8 S&H

[ ] Send *Revelation--Preaching Verse By Verse* By Dr. D. A. Waite ($50+$10 S&H--1030 pages.

[ ] Send *The Occult Connections of Gail Riplinger* by Dr. Phil Stringer ($12.00 + $7.00 S&H).

[ ] Send *A WARNING!! On Gail Riplinger's KJB & Multiple Inspiration HERESY*,133 pp. by Pastor DAW ($12+$7S&H)

[ ] Send *Who Is Gail Riplinger*? 146 pp. by Aleithia O'Brien ($12.00 + $7.00)

[ ] *The Messianic Claims Of Gail A. Riplinger*, By Dr. Phil Stringer, 108 pp., perfect bound ($12.00 + $7.00 S&H)

[ ] Send Husband-Loving Lessons, by Yvonne S. Waite; $25 + $7.00 S&H A very valuable marriage manual

[ ] Send *1 Timothy--Preaching Verse by Verse*, by Pastor D. A. Waite, 288 pages, hardback ($14+$7 S&H) fully indexed.

More Preaching Verse by Verse Books

[ ] Send *Romans--Preaching Verse by Verse* by Pastor D. A. Waite 736 pp. Hardback ($25+$7 S&H) fully indexed

Send or Call Orders to:
THE BIBLE FOR TODAY
900 Park Ave., Collingswood, NJ 08108
Phone: 856-854-4452; FAX:--2464; Orders: 1-800 JOHN 10:9
E-Mail Orders: BFT@BibleForToday.org; Credit Cards OK

Order Blank (p. 3)

Name:_____

Address:_____

City & State:_____Zip:_____

Credit Card #:_____Expires:_____

[ ] Send *8,000 Differences Between Textus Receptus & Critical Text* by Dr.J.A. Moorman, 544 pp., hd.back ($20+$7 S&H)

[ ] *Early Manuscripts, Church Fathers, & the Authorized Version* by Dr. Jack Moorman, $20+$7 S&H. Hardback

[ ] Send *The LIE That Changed the Modern World* by Dr. H. D. Williams ($16+$7 S&H) Hardback book

[ ] Send *With Tears in My Heart* by Gertrude G. Sanborn. Hardback 414 pp. ($25+$7 S&H) 400 Christian Poems

Preaching Verse by Verse Books

[ ] Send *2 Timothy--Preaching Verse by Verse*, by Pastor D. A. Waite, 250 pages, hardback ($11+$7 S&H) fully indexed.

[ ] Send *Colossians & Philemon--Preaching Verse by Verse* by Pastor D. A. Waite ($12+$7 S&H) hardback, 240 pages

[ ] Send *First Peter--Preaching Verse By Verse* by Pastor D. A. Waite ($10+$7 S&H) hardback, 176 pages

[ ] Send *Philippians--Preaching Verse by Verse* by Pastor D. A. Waite ($10+$7 S&H) hardback, 176 pages

[ ] Send *Ephesians--Preaching Verse by Verse* by Pastor D. A. Waite ($12+$7 S&H) hardback, 224 pages

[ ] Send *Galatians--Preaching Verse By Verse* by Pastor D. A. Waite ($13+$7 S&H) hardback, 216 pages

Dr. Waite ($7+$4 S&H) A perfect bound book, 80 pages

[ ] Send *Fuzzy Facts From Fundamentalists* by Dr. D. A. Waite ($8.00 + $7.00 S&H)

Send or Call Orders to:
THE BIBLE FOR TODAY
900 Park Ave., Collingswood, NJ 08108
Phone: 856-854-4452; FAX:--2464; Orders: 1-800 JOHN 10:9
E-Mail Orders: BFT@BibleForToday.org; Credit Cards OK

Order Blank (p. 4)

Name:_____

Address:_____
0
City & State:_____Zip:_____

Credit Card #:_____Expires:_____

More Books on Bible Texts & Translations

[ ] Send *Foes of the King James Bible Refuted* by DAW ($9 +$7 S&H) A perfect bound book, 164 pages in length

[ ] Send *Central Seminary Refuted on Bible Versions* by Dr. Waite ($10+$7 S&H) A perfect bound book, 184 pages

[ ] Send *Defending the King James Bible* by DAW ($12+$7 S&H) A hardback book, indexed with study questions

[ ] Send *BJU's Errors on Bible Preservation* by Dr. D. A. Waite, 110 pages, paperback ($8+$7 S&H) fully indexed

[ ] Send *Fundamentalist Deception on Bible Preservation* by Dr. Waite, ($8+$4 S&H), paperback, fully indexed

[ ] Send *Fundamentalist MIS-INFORMATION on Bible Versions* by Dr. Waite ($7+$5 S&H) perfect bound, 136 pages

[ ] Send *Fundamentalist Distortions on Bible Versions* by

[ ] Send *The Case for the King James Bible* by DAW ($8 +$5 S&H) A perfect bound book, 112 pages in length

[ ] Send *Theological Heresies of Westcott and Hort* by Dr. D. A. Waite, ($8+$5 S&H) A printed booklet

[ ] Send *Westcott's Denial of Resurrection*, Dr. Waite ($8+$5)

[ ] Send *Four Reasons for Defending KJB* by DAW ($4+$3)

More Books on Texts & Translations

[ ] Send *Holes in the Holman Christian Standard Bible* by Dr. Waite ($6+$4 S&H) A printed booklet, 40 pages

Send or Call Orders to:
THE BIBLE FOR TODAY
900 Park Ave., Collingswood, NJ 08108
Phone: 856-854-4452; FAX:--2464; Orders: 1-800 JOHN 10:9
E-Mail Orders: BFT@BibleForToday.org; Credit Cards OK

Order Blank (p. 5)

Name:_____

Address:_____

City & State:_____Zip:_____

Credit Card #:_____Expires:_____
[ ] Send *Contemporary Eng. Version Exposed*, DAW ($6+$4)
   Text" By Dr. Jack Moorman ($17.00 + $7.00 S&H)
More Books By Dr. Jack Moorman
[ ] Send *Missing in Modern Bibles--Nestle/Aland/NIV Errors* by Dr. Jack Moorman, $8+$7 S&H
[ ] Send *The Doctrinal Heart of the Bible--Removed from Modern Versions* by Dr. Jack Moorman, VCR, $15 +$7 S&H
[ ] Send *NIV Inclusive Language Exposed* by DAW ($7+$5)
[ ] Send *24 Hours of KJB Seminar* (4 DVD's) by DAW ($50.00) + $10.00 S&H
Books By Dr. Jack Moorman
[ ] Send *Manuscript Digest of the N.T.* (721 pp.) By Dr. Jack Moorman, copy-machine bound ($50+$10.00 S&H)
[ ] *Early Manuscripts, Church Fathers, & the Authorized Version* by Dr. Jack Moorman, $20+$7 S&H. Hardback
[ ] Send *Forever Settled--Bible Documents & History Survey* by Dr. Jack Moorman, $20+$7 S&H. Hardback book
[ ] Send *When the KJB Departs from the So-Called "Majority*
[ ] Send *Modern Bibles--The Dark Secret* by Dr. Jack Moorman, $5+$4 S&H
[ ] Send *Westcott & Hort's Greek Text & Theory Refuted by Burgon's Revision Revised--Summarized* by Dr. D. A. Waite ($7.00+$5 S&H), 120 pages, perfect bound
[ ] Send *Dean Burgon's Confidence in KJB* by DAW ($5+$4)
[ ] Send *Vindicating Mark 16:9-20* by Dr. Waite ($5+$4 S&H)

Send or Call Orders to:
THE BIBLE FOR TODAY
900 Park Ave., Collingswood, NJ 08108
Phone: 856-854-4452; FAX:--2464; Orders: 1-800 JOHN 10:9
E-Mail Orders: BFT@BibleForToday.org; Credit Cards OK

Order Blank (p. 6)

Name:_____

Address:_____

City & State:_____Zip:_____

Credit Card #:_____Expires:_____

[ ] Send *Samuel P. Tregelles--The Man Who Made the Critical Text Acceptable to Bible Believers* by Dr. Moorman ($5+$3)

[ ] Send *The Traditional Text* hardback by Burgon ($15+$5 S&H) A hardback book, 384 pages in length

[ ] Send *Causes of Corruption* by Burgon ($16+$5 S&H) A hardback book, 360 pages in length

More Books By or About Dean Burgon

[ ] Send *Inspiration and Interpretation*, Dean Burgon ($25+$7 S&H) A hardback book, 610 pages in length

[ ] Send *Burgon's Warnings on Revision* by DAW ($7+$5 S&H) A perfect bound book, 120 pages in length

[ ] Send *8,000 Differences Between TR & CT* by Dr. Jack Moorman [$20 + $7.00 S&H] a hardback book

[ ] Send *The Revision Revised* by Dean Burgon ($25 + $7 S&H) A hardback book, 640 pages in length

[ ] Send *Scrivener's Greek New Testament Underlying the King James Bible*, hardback, ($14 + $7 S&H)

[ ] Send *Scrivener's <u>Annotated</u> Greek New Testament*, by Dr. Frederick Scrivener: Hardback--($35+$7 S&H); Genuine Leather--($45+$7 S&H)

[ ] Send *356 Doctrinal Errors in the NIV & Other Modern Versions*, 100-large-pages, $10.00+$7 S&H

[ ] Send *The Last 12 verses of Mark* by Dean Burgon ($15+$7 S&H) A hardback book 400 pages

Send or Call Orders to:
THE BIBLE FOR TODAY
900 Park Ave., Collingswood, NJ 08108
Phone: 856-854-4452; FAX:--2464; Orders: 1-800 JOHN 10:9
E-Mail Orders: BFT@BibleForToday.org; Credit Cards OK

Order Blank (p. 7)

Name:_____

Address:_____

City & State:_____Zip:_____

Credit Card #:_____Expires:_____

[ ] Send *The Doctored New Testament* by D. A. Waite, Jr. ($25+$7.00 S&H) Greek MSS differences shown, hardback
[ ] Send *Defined King James Bible* lg. prt. leather ($40+$10)
[ ] Send *Defined King James Bible* med. leather $35+$8.50)

Miscellaneous Authors

[ ] Send *The Attack on the Canon of Scripture* by Dr. H. D. Williams, perfect bound ($15.00 + $7.00 S&H)
[ ] Send *Word-For-Word Translating of The Received Texts* by Dr. H. D. Williams, 288 pages, paperback ($10+$7 S&H).
[ ] Send *Guide to Textual Criticism* by Edward Miller ($11+$7 S&H) a hardback book

More Books By or About Dean Burgon

[ ] Send *Summary of Traditional Text* by Dr. Waite ($5 +$4)
[ ] Send *Summary of Causes of Corruption*, DAW ($5+$4)
[ ] Send *Summary of Inspiration* by Dr. Waite ($5+$4 S&H)

More Books by Dr. D. A. Waite

[ ] Send *Making Marriage Melodious* by Pastor D. A. Waite ($7+$5 S&H), perfect bound, 112 pages

Send or Call Orders to:
THE BIBLE FOR TODAY
900 Park Ave., Collingswood, NJ 08108
Phone: 856-854-4452; FAX:--2464; Orders: 1-800 JOHN 10:9
E-Mail Orders: BFT@BibleForToday.org; Credit Cards OK

Order Blank (p. 8)

Name:_____

Address:_____

City & State:_____Zip:_____

Credit Card #:_____Expires:_____

Books by D. A. Waite, Jr.

[ ] Send *Readability of A.V. (KJB)* by D. A. Waite, Jr. ($7+$4)

[ ] Send *4,114 Definitions from the Defined King James Bible* by D. A. Waite, Jr. ($7.00+$5.00 S&H)

Miscellaneous Authors (Continued)

[ ] Send *Why Not the King James Bible?--An Answer to James White's KJVO Book* by Dr. K. D. DiVietro, $10+$7 S&H

[ ] Send Brochure #1: "Over *1000 Titles Defending the KJB/TR*" Compiled by Dr. D. A. Waite. No Charge

Send or Call Orders to:
THE BIBLE FOR TODAY
900 Park Ave., Collingswood, NJ 08108
Phone: 856-854-4452; FAX:--2464; Orders: 1-800 JOHN 10:9
E-Mail Orders: BFT@BibleForToday.org; Credit Cards OK

The Defined King James Bible

Uncommon Words Defined Accurately

I. Deluxe Genuine Leather

✦Large Print--Black or Burgundy✦
1 for $40.00+$10.00 S&H
✦Case of 12 for $360.00✦
$30.00 each+$35 S&H

✦Medium Print--Black or Burgundy✦
1 for $35.00+$8.50 S&H
✦Case of 12 for $300.00✦
$25.00 each+$25 S&H

II. Deluxe Hardback Editions

1 for $20.00+$10.00 S&H (Large Print)
✦Case of 12 for $180.00✦
$15.00 each+$35 S&H (Large Print)
1 for $15.00+$7.50 S&H (Medium Print)
✦Case of 12 for $120.00✦
$10.00 each+$25 S&H (Medium Print)

Able To Bear It   By Gertrude Grace Sanborn

Able To Bear It **By Gertrude Grace Sanborn**

- **The Usefulness of The Book.** May the Lord use *Able To Bear It* to renew your determination to live for the Lord Jesus Christ in spite of any serious problems you might have. You may not be able to escape these problems, but, *"through patience and comfort of the Scriptures,"* you can learn to endure the hurt. Such solace and comfort can be found for you, too, as Gertrude Sanborn discovered it many years ago. Her consolation came in a Book--God's Book--the *Bible*.

- **The Warmth of the Book.** Many parents have children who must face life with unexplained illnesses or deformities. Often that *life of unusualness* falls on the shoulders of the parents and caregivers. That is why *Able to Bear It* has touched the hearts of grieving mothers, fathers, siblings, and grandparents. In the circumstances of her life, the author had experienced every emotion there ever was.

- **The Applications of the Book.** In writing her book, Gertrude Sanborn remembered the stark unbelief she felt when she realized that her little girl was not like other children. She had also faced the years of illness of her firstborn and the death of her second daughter. In His wisdom, her Heavenly Father permitted grief that could not be put into words. Despair encompassed her being. She realized that her only hope for emotional survival was found in the Words of God. So, she put her whole life, and the lives of her three daughters, into God's hand (Psalm 31:15) as she daily immersed herself in God's Words.

www.BibleForToday.org

BFT 4089   **ISBN #978-1-56848-106-7**

www.ingramcontent.com/pod-product-compliance
Lightning Source LLC
Chambersburg PA
CBHW061952070426
42450CB00007BA/1309